COLD MOUNTAIN

Reissued for the
Columbia College Program
of Translations from
the Oriental Classics
Wm. Theodore de Bary, Editor

Han-shan and Shih-te (detail) by Liang K'ai (XIII century)

COLD MOUNTAIN

100 poems
by the T'ang poet
Han-shan

Translated and with an Introduction
by
Burton Watson

COLUMBIA UNIVERSITY PRESS
New York

To Janet and John

*Clothbound editions of Columbia University Press books
are Smyth-sewn and printed on permanent
and durable acid-free paper.*

*Unesco Collection of Representative Works
Chinese Series*
This book
has been accepted
in the Chinese Series
of the Translations Collection
of the United Nations
Educational, Scientific and Cultural Organization
(UNESCO)

First published 1962 by Grove Press
Reissued 1970 by Columbia University Press

Columbia Paperback Edition 1970 Number: 106
International Standard Book Number: 0-231-03450-4 *Paper*
International Standard Book Number: 0-231-03449-0 *Cloth*
p 20 19 18 17 16 15 14 13 12 11 10
Printed in the United States of America

FOREWORD

Cold Mountain (Han-shan) is one of the Translations from the Oriental Classics by which the Committee on Oriental Studies has sought to transmit to Western readers representative works of the major Asian traditions in thought and literature. Our intention is to provide translations based on scholarly study but written for the general reader rather than primarily for other specialists.

The poems of Han-shan are products of the golden age of Chinese poetry and also of the rise of Ch'an (Zen) Buddhism in the T'ang dynasty. Besides having a wide influence on later religious literature in China and Japan, they have been considered among the classics of Chinese poetry generally.

Han-shan has attracted the attention of such translators and poets as Arthur Waley and Gary Snyder, but Professor Watson's selection of one hundred poems, representing about one third of Han-shan's works, is the largest collection so far in English translation. Through this reprinting we hope to keep them available to students of both Chinese literature and Chinese Buddhism.

—*Wm. Theodore de Bary*

INTRODUCTION

Anyone familiar with Chinese or Japanese art has undoubtedly at some time seen pictures of Han-shan, "The Master of Cold Mountain," and his friend Shih-te, "The Foundling"—two grotesque little men guffawing in the wilderness. This image of the two recluses is based upon information contained in the preface to the poems of Han-shan and Shih-te written by an official of the T'ang Dynasty named Lü-ch'iu Yin. Outside of what can be gleaned from the poems themselves, this is the only source we have for the life of Han-shan.

Lü-ch'iu Yin's account begins with the statement that "no one knows where Han-shan came from." It is said, the preface continues, that he was a poor and eccentric scholar who lived in retirement at a place called Cold Cliff in the T'ien-t'ai Mountains, some twenty miles west of the district town of T'ang-hsing. There he often used to go to the Kuo-ch'ing Temple, situated nearby, where a man named Shih-te who worked in the kitchen of the temple would give him bits of leftover food to take home.

After a brief description of Han-shan's ragged dress and unconventional behavior, Lü-ch'iu Yin then relates how he first happened to hear of the recluse. On the eve of his departure for a new post in the vicinity of the T'ien-t'ai Mountains, he was stricken with a severe headache. The doctors he consulted were unable to help him, but a Zen Master named Feng-kan, who had recently left this same Kuo-ch'ing Temple and was traveling in the neighborhood, succeeded in curing it. When Lü-ch'iu Yin asked if there were any worthy teachers at his temple, Feng-kan told him about Han-shan and Shih-te who were in reality, he said, incarnations of the bodhisattvas Manjusri and

Samantabhadra, two prominent deities in the Buddhist pantheon.

After arriving at his new post, Lü-ch'iu Yin went at once to the Kuo-ch'ing Temple to ask about Feng-kan and the two holy men. He was first taken to see the spot where Feng-kan had lived when he was at the temple.

> I then proceeded to the kitchen, where I saw two men standing in front of the stove warming themselves and laughing loudly. I bowed to them, whereupon the two raised their voices in chorus and began to hoot at me. They joined hands and, shrieking with laughter, called out to me, "Blabbermouth blabbermouth Feng-kan! You wouldn't even know the Buddha Amitabha if you saw him! What do you mean by bowing to us?"
>
> The monks all came rushing in and gathered around, astonished that a high official like myself should be bowing to two such poor men. Then the two joined hands and dashed out of the temple. I sent someone after them, but they ran too fast and had soon returned to Cold Cliff.

Lü-ch'iu Yin later dispatched men with presents of clothing and medicine for the hermits, but when Han-shan saw the gift-bearers coming he shouted "Thieves! thieves!" and vanished into a cave, which closed after him. Shih-te likewise disappeared. Lü-ch'iu Yin then enlisted the aid of the monks in gathering together a number of poems which Han-shan had inscribed "on trees and rocks or the walls of the houses and offices in the nearby village," as well as some poems of Shih-te, until he had made up a collection of over three hundred poems.

And when did all this take place? Lü-ch'iu Yin gives no indication, and his preface, contrary to Chinese custom, is undated. Lü-ch'iu Yin represents himself as a high official and prefixes his name with a very imposing title. But there is only one mention of anyone by this name to be found in other works of the period, and it refers almost certainly to another person. This fact alone is peculiar enough, if Lü-ch'iu Yin was in fact as high up in the bureaucracy as his title indicates. Furthermore, the style of the preface, awkward and wordy, hardly suggests the writing of an eminent official. All other sources that tell us anything about Han-shan and Shih-te appear to be later than the preface and based upon it. For all we know, therefore, the whole picture of the two recluses built up in the preface may be nothing more than a literary fiction.

The poems, however, remain—over three hundred of them, as Lü-ch'iu Yin says, most of them attributed to Han-shan, a few to Shih-te and Feng-kan (none of the latter translated here). If the reader wishes to know the biography of Han-shan, he must deduce it from the poems themselves.

Though some of the poems in the collection are probably later additions, a large part of them appears to be by one man, a gentleman farmer, troubled by poverty and family discord, who, after extensive wandering and perhaps a career as a minor official, retired to a place called Cold Mountain among the T'ien-t'ai range. In one poem he says he went to Cold Mountain at the age of thirty, and in another he speaks of having lived there thirty years; these are the only bits of information we have on the chronology of his life. Scholars, with no real evidence to go by, have suggested a variety of dates for the poet's lifetime, ranging from the late sixth to the late ninth century. The most recent hypothesis, based on internal evidence of the poems and the fact that no reference to them is found before the ninth century, places him in the late eighth and early ninth centuries. This is the dating followed by Arthur Waley and Yoshitaka Iriya (see Translator's Note), and for readers who like their poets neatly chronologized I suggest this pigeonhole, with the understanding that it is provisional and subject to the changes of academic fashion.

The poems deal with a remarkable range of subjects. Some are fairly conventional laments on the shortness of life; others are complaints of poverty or biting satires on avarice and pride. There are accounts of the hardships of official life under the Chinese bureaucratic system, attacks on the worldly Buddhist clergy, and ridicule of the fatuous attempts of the Taoist alchemists and devotees to achieve immortal life. And finally there are the incomparable descriptions of Han-shan's mountain retreat and his life there. These vivid delineations of the natural world which are at the same time allegories of spiritual questing and attainment are the poems that have made his name famous in China and Japan. Arthur Waley, in the introduction to his translations of Han-shan, has written of these poems: "Cold Mountain is often the name of a state of mind rather than a locality. It is on this conception, as well as on that of the 'hidden treasure,' the Buddha who is to be sought not somewhere outside us, but 'at home' in the heart, that the mysticism of the poems is based." (*Encounter*, Vol. III, No. 3, September, 1954.)

Buddhism had a dramatically vitalizing effect upon Chinese art, inspiring centuries of glorious sculpture, architecture, and painting. Its influence on Chinese literature was less spectacular—in fact, particularly in the field of poetry, decidedly disappointing. Since China already had a long and well developed tradition of lyric, rhapsodic, and descriptive poetry when Buddhism was

introduced in the first century A.D., one would expect to
see the piety and intellectual excitement which the new
religion aroused in China translated into superb poetry.
But Chinese Buddhism produced no *Pearl* or *Paradise
Lost*, no Dante or Donne. True, there is an enormous
body of Buddhist poetry in Chinese. But it is for the most
part no more than rhymed sermonizing, seldom rising
above doggerel; for all its doctrinal importance, its literary value has been customarily rated—and rightly so,
I think—rather low.

In the works of most first-rate Chinese poets, Buddhism figures very slightly, usually as little more than
a vague mood of resignation or a picturesque embellish-
ment in the landscape—the mountain temple falling into
melancholy ruin, the old monk one visits on an outing
in the hills. Han-shan, however, is a striking exception
to this rule. The collection of poetry attributed to him
contains a certain number of sermons in doggerel—the
sin of meat-eating is one of the most frequent themes—
though they may not be from his hand at all. But it also
contains a large proportion of excellent poetry which is
permeated with deep and compelling religious feeling.
For this reason he holds a place of special importance in
Chinese literature. He proved that it was possible to
write great poetry on Buddhist, as well as Confucian and
Taoist, themes; that the cold abstractions of Mahayana
philosophy could be transformed into personal and im-
passioned literature. The surprising thing is that so few
of his countrymen ever felt inclined to explore the paths
he opened.

The language of his poems is simple, often colloquial
or even slangy (the slang of a thousand years ago, all but
unintelligible today). Many of his images and terms are
drawn from the Buddhist sutras or the sayings of the

Southern School of Zen, whose doctrine of the Buddha as present in the minds of all men—of Buddha as the mind itself—he so often refers to. At the same time he is solidly within the Chinese poetic tradition, his language again and again echoing the works of earlier poets, particularly the eremitic poets of the preceding Six Dynasties era. All the poems translated here employ the conventional five-character line, and consist usually of eight lines. The even numbered lines rhyme, the same rhyme being used throughout a single poem. Some are in the rather free "old poetry" style; others in the more exacting *lü-shih* or "regulated verse" form, with its elaborate verbal and tonal parallelisms.

The poems are arranged somewhat differently in different editions and, since they seem from the beginning to have had no fixed order, I have taken the liberty of making may own arrangement in the translation. I began with some poems that clearly deal with the poet's early life, along with some conventional romantic lyrics. These are followed by satires and poems showing the writer's increasing disgust with the world, many of them marked by considerable spleen and self-pity. Some of these picture the poet as already an old man and may not be by Han-shan at all. Next come the poems on his retirement to Cold Mountain, his experiences there, and the alternating moods of elation and despair which beset him. The selection closes with a group of poems on Buddhist themes. All the poems are untitled. As Iriya remarks, it is up to the reader himself to supply titles.

Mount T'ien-t'ai, the location of Cold Mountain, is a range of mountains stretching along the seacoast in the northeastern corner of Chekiang Province, south of the Bay of Hangchow. The mountains, famous for their wild and varied scenery, were from early times venerated as the home of spirits and immortals, and from the third century on became the site of numerous Taoist and Buddhist monasteries.

It might be well to add here a word on the interpretation of the poems which I have adopted. Han-shan has traditionally been regarded as essentially a Buddhist—or more specifically a Zen—poet, and surely the frequent allusions to the sutras in his work, the typically Buddhist terminology, the references to "sitting," would seem to justify this view (though Taoist-inclined critics have attempted, on the basis of Taoist references, to claim him for their side). If we accept the dating suggested above, it means that he lived at a time when Chinese Zen was in its period of greatest creative activity, a period when many fervent Buddhists, repelled by the formalism and aristocratic-mindedness of earlier T'ang Buddhism, preferred to remain as *chü-shih* or "lay believers" rather than become members of the clergy. On the basis of the information in Lü-ch'iu Yin's preface, Han-shan has therefore been venerated, particularly in Japan, as a typical example of the carefree, enlightened Zen layman. The commentaries on his poems, all by Japanese Zen monks, have worked out the implications of this view in detail.

While this interpretation is probably basically sound, it has led to some rather forced readings of the poems. An example is the word "sitting" in the poems: in some or even all instances it may, as the commentators say, refer to *zazen*—the particular Zen method of meditation —but on the other hand it may equally well mean no more than just plain sitting. On a larger and

more serious scale, the commentators have been forced
to resort to some drastic wrenching in their interpreta-
tions of the poems by the fact that Han-shan, though
at times speaking from a pinnacle of calm and enlightenment, just as often seems to be profoundly involved
in the misgivings and anxieties that enlightenment is
supposed to dispel. Christian saints may be permitted
their lapses of faith, but in Zen, with its strong empha-
sis on individual effort and self-reliance, a man, once
enlightened, is expected to stay that way. Zen commentators have therefore been forced to regard Han-shan's
professions of loneliness, doubt, and discouragement
not as revelations of his own feelings but as vicarious
recitals of the ills of unenlightened men which he can
still sympathize with, though he himself has tran-
scended them. He thus becomes in effect the traditional
bodhisattva figure—compassionate, in the world, but
not of it.

Following Iriya, I have declined to accept this view.
If poets must be consistent, then some such interpretation is obviously necessary, particularly if one is to accept the picture of Han-shan, the laughing recluse,
built up in Lü-ch'iu Yin's preface, and reconcile it with
the poems themselves. Personally I prefer to read the
poems as a chronicle of spiritual search—rewarded at
times by moments of wonderful contentment, but at
other times frustrated by loneliness and despair—
rather than as a pat report of success.

—*Burton Watson*

TRANSLATOR'S NOTE

By rights, two names should appear as translators of this volume. Though the English of the poems is entirely my own responsibility, I would hardly have had the temerity to undertake this translation if it had not been for the recently published work on Han-shan by Yoshitaka Iriya, Professor of Chinese Literature of Nagoya University and a member of the Kyoto University Research Institute of Humanistic Studies. In 1958 Iriya brought out a selection of the poems of Han-shan, containing an introduction on the problem of Han-shan's identity, Japanese translations of 126 poems, and exhaustive notes. Entitled *Kanzan*, the volume is No. 5 of the *Chūgoku shijin senshū* series ("Selected Works of Chinese Poets"), edited by Professors Kōjirō Yoshikawa and Tamaki Ogawa of Kyoto University and published by the Iwanami Shoten in Tokyo. With his thorough knowledge of the colloquial literature of the T'ang period, Iriya has offered a number of new suggestions on the reading and interpretation of the poems, and it is his work which has formed the basis of my English versions. I have translated about ninety of the poems in his selection, adding some others which he did not include but which he has gone over with me. For the interpretation of the poems, many of the notes, and much of the material in the introduction, therefore, I am indebted to him.

I am also indebted to the translations of twenty-seven of Han-shan's poems by Arthur Waley, published in *Encounter*, Vol. III, No. 3, September, 1954, and to those of Gary Snyder in the *Evergreen Review*, Vol. II, No. 6, Autumn, 1958, for many suggestions on rendering Han-shan into English. Readers interested in Han-shan should by all means consult these translations, which include some poems not contained in my selection. Further translations and an exhaustive discussion of the dating of the poems will be found in Wu Chi-yu, "A Study of Han Shan," *T'oung Pao* 45, 4–5, 1957. A masterful finding list coordinating all these translations, including my own, with the Chinese originals, has been compiled by David Hawkes and appears in *Journal of the American Oriental Society* 82.4, 1962, 597–599.

I would like to take this opportunity to thank Professor Chiang Yee of Columbia University, who kindly wrote the Chinese title for me; the Harvard-Yenching Institute for its grant to subsidize original publication; and the many other friends who read this manuscript and made valuable suggestions for improvement.

—B. W.

New York
April, 1970

COLD MOUNTAIN

1

My father and mother left me a good living;
I need not envy the fields of other men.
Clack—clack—my wife works her loom,
Jabber, jabber, goes my son at play.
I clap hands, urging on the swirling petals,
Chin in hand, I listen to singing birds.
Who comes to commend me on my way of life?
Well, the woodcutter sometimes passes by.

2

A thatched hut is home for a country man;
Horse or carriage seldom pass my gate:
Forests so still all the birds come to roost,
Broad valley streams always full of fish.
I pick wild fruit in hand with my child,
Till the hillside fields with my wife.
And in my house what do I have?
Only a bed piled high with books.

3

In the third month, when the silkworms
                    are still small,
Girls come, picking flowers.
Leaning against the wall, they play with
                    butterflies;
Down by the river, they throw pebbles at a frog.
They fill their gauze sleeves with plums;
With golden hairpins they dig bamboo shoots.
Debate all you want on the nature of beauty,*
This place is finer than the one where I live!

* The meaning of the line is doubtful.

4

Above the blossoms sing the orioles:
Kuan kuan, their clear notes.
The girl with a face like jade
Strums to them on her lute.
Never does she tire of playing—
Youth is the time for tender thoughts.
When the flowers scatter and the birds fly off
Her tears will fall in the spring wind.

5

"Han-tan* is my home," she said,
"And the lilt of the place is in my songs.
Living here so long
I know all the old tunes handed down.
You're drunk? Don't say you're going home!
Stay! The sun hasn't reached its height.
In my bedroom is an embroidered quilt
So big it covers all my silver bed!"

* The capital of the ancient state of
Chao, noted for its beautiful women
and its songs and dances.

6

I call to my friends, picking lotus,
Wonderfully afloat on the clear river,
And forget, in my delight, how late it grows,
Till gusts of evening wind whirl by.
Waves scoop up the mandarin ducks;
Ripples rock the broad-tailed mallards;
At this moment, sitting in my boat,
Thoughts pour out in endless streams.

7

You have seen the blossoms among the leaves;
Tell me, how long will they stay?
Today they tremble before the hand that
                                picks them;
Tomorrow they wait someone's garden broom.
Wonderful is the bright heart of youth,
But with the years it grows old.
Is the world not like these flowers?
Ruddy faces, how can they last?

8

Young as he was, Lord Tung*
Came and went in the Emperor's palace.
His blouse was the pale yellow of gosling down;
His face and figure were as fine as a painting.
Always he rode a snow-footed horse,
Whirling, whirling up the red dust,
And the people who lined the roads to watch
Would ask each other, "Whose son is this?"

* Tung Hsien was a favorite of Emperor
Ai (reigned 6-1 B.C.) of the Former Han
Dynasty and, because of imperial pa-
tronage, succeeded in accumulating a
fortune and winning high office in the
government. It is said that once when
the Emperor rose early in the morning
to attend court, he cut off the sleeve of
his robe so as not to wake the young
man who slept by his side. When the
Emperor died soon after, however, the
chief minister Wang Mang forced Tung
Hsien to commit suicide.

9

A curtain of pearls hangs before the hall of jade,
And within is a lovely lady,
Fairer in form than the gods and immortals,
Her face like a blossom of peach or plum.
Spring mists will cover the eastern mansion,
Autumn winds blow from the western lodge,
And after thirty years have passed,
She will look like a piece of pressed sugar cane.

10

Here we languish, a bunch of poor scholars,
Battered by extremes of hunger and cold.
Out of work, our only joy is poetry:
Scribble, scribble, we wear out our brains.
Who will read the works of such men?
On that point you can save your sighs.
We could inscribe our poems on biscuits
And the homeless dogs wouldn't deign to nibble.

11

Man's life is less than a hundred years,
But he is saddled with a thousand years' woes.
No sooner have you cured a sickness of your own
Than your sons and grandsons load you with care.
Stoop down to see how your grain is growing,
Look up to examine your mulberry trees—
When the scale weights have plunked to the
                    bottom of the sea,
Only then will you have a moment to rest.

12

If you have wine, call me in to drink;
When I have meat, come feast with me.
All bound for the Yellow Springs   sooner or later,
We must work while we're young and strong.
Jeweled belts glitter but a little while;
Golden hairpins won't be needed long.
Did you know about Father Chang and
                    old lady Cheng?
They went away and no one's heard from them
                    since.

13

Some people are always bragging of their conduct:
"Confucius or the Duke of Chou could not match
  my talents!"
Yet look at their heads, stubborn and stony!
See their bodies, ungainly and stiff!
Pull them by a rope and they refuse to move;
Poke them with an awl and they won't budge.
There they stand, like Mr. Yang's stork,
Born, I'm afraid, to be as dull as clods!*

* A man named Yang Shu-tzu had a stork which was very clever at dancing. When he boasted of the bird's talents to a friend, the friend requested a demonstration. Mr. Yang eagerly led forth his stork, but the bird only stood there, "dull as a clod," and refused to perform. (Shih-shuo hsin-yü, P'ai-tiao Chapter.)

14

Here's a man with a good head and belly;
He's mastered every one of the Six Arts.*
But when he sets out southward, he gets chased
                              north;
When he starts off westward, he gets chased east,
Like the duckweed, forever drifting,
Blown on without rest like tumbleweed.
What sort of fellow is this, you ask?
His last name is Poor and his first name Trouble.

* The six polite arts of the Chinese gentleman: etiquette, music, archery, charioteering, calligraphy, and mathematics.

15

The wife of Lord Tsou of Ti-yen,
The mother of Scholar Tu of Han-tan,
Both of them well along in years,
Both of them women with pleasant faces,
Yesterday happened to go to a party,
But, their clothes being shabby, they were shown
                      to the rear.
Only because their hems were frayed,
They got nothing to eat but some leftover cake.

16

Aah! poverty and sickness,
And me with no friends or relations.
There's never any rice left in the pot,
Dust often collects in the kettle.
A thatched roof that won't keep out the rain,
A broken-down bed I can hardly squeeze into,
No wonder I've gotten so thin—
This many worries would wear out any man!

17

This month, when farmers stay indoors to shun
the heat,
Who will drink with me and be merry?
Here I lay out a handful of mountain fruit,
But gathered about the wine jar is no one but me.
Rushes serve in place of a mat;
A plantain leaf will do for a plate.
After I'm drunk, I sit with chin in hand,
And Sumeru* seems no bigger than a crossbow
pellet!

* The great mountain that stands at the
center of the Buddhist universe.

18

North of the city lived old man Chung;
His larder was full of meat and wine.
Ah, the day his poor wife died
The funeral guests overflowed the hall.
But when old man Chung himself passed on,
Not a single soul came to weep.
Those who ate his roasts and downed his wine
Had hearts that were colder than you would have
thought!

19

I'm not so poor at reports and decisions—
Why can't I get ahead in the government?
The rating officials are determined to make life
                    hard.
All they do is try to expose my faults.
Everything, I guess, is a matter of Fate;
Still, I'll try the exam again this year.
A blind boy aiming at the eye of a sparrow
Might just accidentally manage a hit.

20

As long as I was living in the village
They said I was the finest man around,
But yesterday I went to the city
And even the dogs eyed me askance.
Some people jeered at my skimpy trousers,
Others said my jacket was too long.
If someone would poke out the eyes of the hawks
We sparrows could dance wherever we please!

21

When I see a fellow abusing others,
I think of a man with a basketful of water.
As fast as he can, he runs with it home,
But when he gets there, what's left in the basket?
When I see a man being abused by others,
I think of the leek growing in the garden.
Day after day men pull off the leaves,
But the heart it was born with stays the same.

22

Elegant is the bearing of the fine young man;
He is widely read in the classics and history.
Everyone addresses him as "Professor";
Everyone refers to him as "the scholar."
Yet he hasn't been able to get a government job
And he doesn't know how to handle a hoe.
All winter he shivers in his worn hemp shirt:
"My books have brought me to a pretty pass!"

23

In the house east of here lives an old woman.
Three or four years ago, she got rich.
In the old days she was poorer than I;
Now she laughs at me for not having a penny.
She laughs at me for being behind;
I laugh at her for getting ahead.
We laugh as though we'd never stop:
She from the east and I from the west!

24

I used to be fairly poor, as poor goes;
Today I hit the bottom of poverty and cold.
Nothing I do seems to come out right;
Wherever I go I get pushed around.
I walk the muddy road and my footsteps falter;
I sit with the other villagers and my stomach
                                 aches with hunger.
Since I lost the brindle cat,
The rats come right up and peer into the pot.

25

The new grain hasn't ripened yet,
But today I used up the last of the old.
I went out to borrow a measureful
And stood at their gate, hesitating.
The husband came to the door and said
               to speak to his wife;
The wife came out and said "Ask my husband!"
Too stingy to help when times are bad—
The more the wealth, the bigger the fool!

26

They laugh at me for being a hick—
"Did you ever see such a stupid expression?
His cap won't even stand up right!
Does he always wear his belt pulled in like that?"
It's not that I don't know the fashions,
But when you're broke you can't keep up.
One day when I get a lot of money
I'll have a hat as high as that pagoda there!

27

Wise men may be free of greed,
But not the fool, who loves to dig for gold.
His fields encroach on his neighbors' lands;
And the bamboo grove? "This is all mine!"
See him elbow his way in search of money,
Gnash his teeth and drive his horses and slaves—
Look there, beyond the city gates,
How many grave mounds under the pines!

28

A certain scholar named Mr. Wang
Was laughing at my poems for being so clumsy.
"Don't you know you can't have two accents here?
And this line has too many beats.*
You don't seem to understand meter at all
But toss in any word that comes to mind!"
I laugh too, Mr. Wang, when *you* make a poem,
Like a blind man trying to sing of the sun.

* Literally, Mr. Wang accuses Han-shan
of committing two faults of meter desig-
nated in the technical language of Chinese poetics as "wasp's waist" and
"stork's knees."

29

I spur my horse past the ruined city;
The ruined city, that wakes the traveler's thoughts:
Ancient battlements, high and low;
Old grave mounds, great and small.
Where the shadow of a single tumbleweed
                    trembles
And the voice of the great trees clings forever,
I sigh over all these common bones—
No roll of the immortals bears their names.

30

In vain I slaved to understand the Three Histories;
Uselessly I pored over the Five Classics.
Until I'm old I'll go on checking census figures;
As in the past, a petty clerk scribbling in
                tax ledgers.
When I ask the *I Ching* it says there's
                trouble ahead;
All my life is ruled by evil stars.
If only I could be like the tree at the river's edge
Every year turning green again!

31

A crowd of girls playing in the dusk,
And a wind-blown fragrance that fills the road!
Golden butterflies are sewn to the hems of their
skirts;
Their chignons are pinned with mandarin ducks
of jade.
Their maids wear cloaks of sheer crimson silk;
Purple brocade for the eunuchs who attend them.
Will they give a glance to one who's lost the way,
With hair turned white and a restless heart?

32

I took along books when I hoed the fields,*
In my youth, when I lived with my older brother.
Then people began to talk;
Even my wife turned against me.
Now I've broken my ties with the world of red dust;
I spend my time wandering and read all I want.
Who will lend a dipper of water
To save a fish in a carriage rut?†

* From the story of an impoverished
scholar of the Former Han Dynasty
who was so fond of learning that he
carried his copies of the Confucian
Classics along when he went to work
in the fields. (*Han shu* 58, biography
of Ni K'uan.)
† An allusion to the perch, stranded in
a carriage rut in the road, who asked
the philosopher Chuang Tzu for a dip-
perful of water so that he could go on
living. (*Chuang Tzu*, sec. 26.)

33

Once I was a student with books and sword;
I have lived under two enlightened sovereigns.
I was an official in the east, but they gave me
                    no prizes;
I fought in the west but won no medals.
I studied the arts of peace and the arts of war,
The arts of war and the arts of peace.
Now I'm an old man.
What's left of my life isn't worth mentioning.

34

The rich man feasted in his high hall,
Bright torches shining everywhere,
When a man too poor to own a lamp
Crept to the side to share in the glow.
Who would think they would drive him away,
Back again to his place in the dark?
"Will one more person detract from your light?
Strange, to begrudge me a leftover beam!"

35

I think a lot about the days of my youth
When I went hunting in the broad uplands.
I had no wish for government jobs;
You couldn't have tempted me with the
                    life of the gods.
Galloping like the wind on my white horse,
I shouted at the hares and loosed my hawks
                    on them.
Then, before I knew it, things went to pieces.
Now who would bother with an old man?

36

Why am I always so depressed?
Man's life is like the morning mushroom.*
Who can bear, in a few dozen years,
To see new friends and old all gone away?
Thinking of this, I am filled with sadness,
A sadness I can hardly endure.
What shall I do? Say, what shall I do?
Take this old body home and hide it in the
         mountains!

* The little mushroom that springs up
in the morning and shrivels away before nightfall. (*Chuang Tzu*, sec. 1.)

37

I think of all the places I've been,
Chasing about from one famous spot to another.
Delighting in mountains, I scaled the mile high
                    peaks;
Loving the water, I sailed a thousand rivers.
I held farewell parties with my friends in
                    Lute Valley;
I brought my zither and played on Parrot Shoals.
Who would guess I'd end up under a pine tree,
Clasping my knees in the whispering cold?

starts with general
evidence

gets more specific
to focus on one

38

Thirty years ago I was born into the world.
A thousand, ten thousand miles I've roamed,
By rivers where the green grass lies thick,
Beyond the border where the red sands fly.
I brewed potions in a vain search for
                    life everlasting,
I read books, I sang songs of history,
And today I've come home to Cold Mountain
To pillow my head on the stream and
                    wash my ears.*

* When Sun Ch'u, an official of the third
century A.D., was about to retire to the
wilderness, he intended to tell a friend
that he was going to "pillow his head
on a stone and rinse his mouth in the
stream." He got mixed up, however, and
announced instead that he was going
to "pillow his head on a stream and
rinse his mouth with a stone." Chal-
lenged to explain this curious statement,
he replied, "By pillowing my head on a
stream I can wash my ears, and by rins-
ing my mouth with a stone I can polish
my teeth!" (*Shih-shuo hsin-yü, Yen-yü*
Chapter.) The washing of the ears refers
to a much older story of the sage recluse Hsü Yu who, when asked by Emperor Yao to take over the throne, hast-
ily went and washed his ears to cleanse
them of such a vile suggestion.

39

The birds and their chatter overwhelm me
               with feeling:
At times like this I lie down in my straw hut.
Cherries shine with crimson fire;
Willows trail slender boughs.
The morning sun pops from the jaws of blue peaks;
Bright clouds are washed in the green pond.
Who ever thought I would leave the dusty world
And come bounding up the southern slope of
               Cold Mountain?

40

I climb the road to Cold Mountain,
The road to Cold Mountain that never ends.
The valleys are long and strewn with stones;
The streams broad and banked with thick grass.
Moss is slippery, though no rain has fallen;
Pines sigh, but it isn't the wind.
Who can break from the snares of the world
And sit with me among the white clouds?

41

Where white clouds pile on jagged peaks
And the green pond stirs with ripples,
In this place I hear a fisherman
Now and then dip his oar and sing:
His voice, and then his voice again,
                    until I cannot listen;
It makes my thoughts too sad.
"Who says the sparrow has no horn?
See how he pokes a hole in the roof!"*

*From the *Book of Odes*, Airs of Shao-
nan, *Hsing-lu*:

  Who says the sparrow has no horn?
  How has he poked a hole in my roof?

That is, though the fisherman bears me
no ill will, his songs poke holes of sadness in me.

42

I lie alone by folded cliffs,
Where churning mists even at midday do not part.
Though it is dark here in the room,
My mind is clear and free of clamor.
In dreams I roam past golden portals;
My spirit returns across the stone bridge.
I have thrust aside everything that vexes me—
Clatter! clatter! goes the dipper in the tree.*

* Someone, feeling sorry for the hermit
Hsü Yu because he had to drink water
from his hands, gave him a gourd dipper. But after using it once, Hsü Yu hung
it in a tree and went off, leaving it to
clatter in the wind.

43

I divined and chose a distant place to dwell—
T'ien-t'ai: what more is there to say?
Monkeys cry where valley mists are cold;
My grass gate blends with the color of the crags.
I pick leaves to thatch a hut among the pines,
Scoop out a pond and lead a runnel from the spring.
By now I am used to doing without the world.
Picking ferns, I pass the years that are left.*

* From the story of the brothers Po-i
and Shu-ch'i who, angered at the conduct of the founder of the Chou Dynasty, retired to Mount Shou-yang,
where they lived on ferns until they
died of starvation.

44

Story on story of wonderful hills and streams,
Their blue-green haze locked in clouds!
Mists brush my thin cap with moisture,
Dew wets my coat of plaited straw.
On my feet I wear pilgrim's sandals,
My hand holds a stick of old rattan.
Though I look down again on the dusty world,
What is that land of dreams to me?

45

Cold Mountain is full of weird sights;
People who try to climb it always get scared.
When the moon shines, the water glints and
                         sparkles;
When the wind blows, the grasses rustle and sigh.
Snowflakes make blossoms for the bare plum,
Clouds in place of leaves for the naked trees.
At a touch of rain, the whole mountain shimmers—
But only in good weather can you make the climb.

46

The place where I spend my days
Is farther away than I can tell.
Without a wind the wild vines stir;
No fog, yet the bamboos are always dark.
Who do the valley streams sob for?
Why do the mists huddle together?
At noon, sitting in my hut,
I realize for the first time that the sun has risen.

47

How cold it is on the mountain!
Not just this year but always.
Crowded peaks forever choked with snow,
Dark forests breathing endless mist:
No grass sprouts till the early days of June;
Before the first of autumn, leaves are falling.
And here a wanderer, drowned in delusion,
Looks and looks but cannot see the sky.

obstacles

Try to see truth, can't.

Depressed.

Down on pursuit of Enlightenment

48

Wonderful, this road to Cold Mountain—
Yet there's no sign of horse or carriage.
In winding valleys too tortuous to trace,
On crags piled who knows how high,
A thousand different grasses weep with dew
And pines hum together in the wind.
Now it is that, straying from the path,
You ask your shadow, "What way from here?"

No one else follows the Way (Tao)

If you get lost in valley, you are really alone, left on your own. [ask your shadow]

49

As for me, I delight in the everyday Way,*
Among mist-wrapped vines and rocky caves.
Here in the wilderness I am completely free,
With my friends, the white clouds, idling forever.
There are roads, but they do not reach the world;
Since I am mindless,† who can rouse my thoughts?
On a bed of stone I sit, alone in the night,
While the round moon climbs up Cold Mountain.

Very Zen

Her only Friend

No thought

Enlightenment Enlightened mind

* A reference perhaps to the words attributed to the Zen Master Ma-tsu Tao-i
(707-786): "The everyday mind—that
is the Way." (Ching-te ch'uan-teng lu
28, biography of Nan-ch'üan.)
† Wu-hsin, a Buddhist term indicating
the state in which all ordinary processes
of discriminatory thinking have been
stilled.

[67]

50

If you're looking for a place to rest,
Cold Mountain is good for a long stay.
The breeze blowing through the dark pines
Sounds better the closer you come.
And under the trees a white-haired man
Mumbles over his Taoist texts.
Ten years now he hasn't gone home;
He's even forgotten the road he came by.

51

I sit alone in constant fret,
Pressed by endless thoughts and feelings.
Clouds hang about the waist of the mountain,
Wind moans in the valley mouth.
Monkeys come, shaking the branches;
A bird flies into the wood with shrill cries.
Seasons pass and my hair grows ragged and grey;
Year's end finds me old and desolate.

52

Last year, in the spring, when the birds
               were calling,
I thought of my brothers and kin.
This year, when fall chrysanthemums bloom,
I remember the time of my youth,
When green waters murmured in a thousand
               streams
And yellow clouds filled the sky.
Ah, all the hundred years of my life
Must I recall with such heartache those days
               in the capital?

53

If you sit in silence and never speak,
What stories will you leave for the young people
                              to tell?
If you live shut away in a forest thicket,
How can the sun of wisdom shine out?
No dried-up carcass can be the guardian
                    of the Way.
Wind and frost bring sickness and early death.
Plow with a clay ox in a field of stone
And you will never see the harvest day!

54

You cannot take my will and roll it up;
You should know that I am not a mat!*
Freely I came to this mountain forest
To lie down alone on a rocky bed.
And now these artful talkers come to plead with me
And beg me to accept their gold and jewels.†
Poking holes in the wall to plant weeds in them—
This is no help to anyone!‡

* A reference to the *Book of Odes*,
Airs of Pei, *Po-chou*:

"My heart is not a stone
  to be tumbled about;
My heart is not a mat
  to be rolled up."

†From the story of how King Hsiang
of Ch'u sent envoys with gifts of gold
and jewels in an unsuccessful attempt
to persuade the philosopher Chuang
Tzu to leave his retirement and become chief minister of the state.

‡ One of Lao Tzu's disciples criticized
the sage rulers Yao and Shun of antiq-
uity, saying that they did no more
than poke holes in the wall (of original simplicity) to plant weeds (of conventional morality). (*Chuang Tzu*, sec.
23.)

55

Cold cliffs, more beautiful the deeper you enter—
Yet no one travels this road.
White clouds idle about the tall crags;
On the green peak a single monkey wails.
What other companions do I need?
I grow old doing as I please.
Though face and form alter with the years,
I hold fast to the pearl of the mind.*

* In the *Fourteen Hymns* of the Liang
Dynasty priest Pao-chih (418-514) are
the lines:

> Why should you look
>   for treasure abroad?
> Within yourself you
>   have a bright pearl!

The pearl is the Buddha-nature within
the mind of every person.

56

Reading books won't save you from death;
Reading books won't save you from poverty.
Then why do people want to be literate?
To be that much ahead of everyone else!
A young man who can't read characters
Will never get along in the world today.
Try mixing your medicine with garlic sauce
And you'll soon forget the bitter-and-the-bite.*

* That is, the sauce of learning will help
you to forget the bitter-and-the-bite of
life. "Medicine"—literally *huang-lien*
or *Coptis japonica*, the bitter root of
which is used in many Chinese medi-
cines.

[74]

57

When people see the man of Cold Mountain
They all say, "There's a crackpot!
Hardly a face to make one look twice,
His body wrapped in nothing but rags . . .
The things we say he doesn't understand;
The things he says we wouldn't utter!"
A word to those of you passing by—
Try coming to Cold Mountain sometime!

58

The peach blossoms would like to stay through
               the summer
But winds and moons hurry them on and
               will not wait.
Though you look for the men of the Han Dynasty
Not a one will you find alive.
Morning after morning flowers fade and fall;
Year after year men pass away.
Here, where the dust whirls up today,
In times gone by was a sprawling sea.

59

In the old days when I was so poor,
Night after night I counted other men's wealth.
Recently I thought it over
And decided to open a business of my own.
I dug a hole and found a hidden treasure—
A store of crystal jewels.
A blue-eyed foreigner came in secret*
And wanted to buy them and take them away,
But I only answered him,
"These jewels are beyond price!"

* That is, a merchant from Central Asia;
"in secret"—to avoid the notice of the
government officials.

60

I look far off at T'ien-t'ai's summit,
Alone and high above the crowding peaks.
Pines and bamboos sing in the wind that
                    sways them;
Sea tides wash beneath the shining moon.
I gaze at the mountain's green borders below
And discuss philosophy with the white clouds.
In the wilderness, mountains and seas are all right,
But I wish I had a companion in my search
                    for the Way.

61

Among a thousand clouds and ten thousand
                              streams,
Here lives an idle man,
In the daytime wandering over green mountains,
At night coming home to sleep by the cliff.
Swiftly the springs and autumns pass,
But my mind is at peace, free from dust or delusion.
How pleasant, to know I need nothing to lean on,
To be still as the waters of the autumn river!

62

High, high from the summit of the peak,
Whatever way I look, no limit in sight!
No one knows I am sitting here alone.
A solitary moon shines in the cold spring.
Here in the spring—this is not the moon.
The moon is where it always is—in the sky above.
And though I sing this one little song,
In the song there is no Zen.

63

Last night in a dream I returned to my old home
And saw my wife weaving at her loom.
She held her shuttle poised, as though lost
                    in thought,
As though she had no strength to lift it further.
I called. She turned her head to look,
But her eyes were blank—she didn't know me.
So many years we've been parted
The hair at my temples has lost its old color.

64

Be happy if there's something to be happy about!
When the moment comes, do not lose it!
Though they say life lasts a hundred years,
Who has seen a full thirty thousand days?
You're in this world no more than an instant,
So don't sit there grumbling about money.
At the end of the *Classic of Filial Piety**
It tells you all about what funerals are like.

* A short work on ethics and filial conduct which was popular among the common people of this period.

65

Yesterday I saw the trees by the river's edge,
Wrecked and broken beyond belief,
Only two or three trunks left standing,
Scarred by blades of a thousand axes.
Frost strips the yellowing leaves,
River waves pluck at withered roots.
This is the way the living must fare.
Why curse at Heaven and Earth?

66

In the beginning, He parted heaven and earth
And set man down to live in the middle.
He belched forth fog to bewilder us,
And sent the wind to wake us up.
When He's kind, He gives us wealth and honor,
And when He's mean, it's trouble and want.
Listen, you fellows banging around down here—
Everything depends on the Man Upstairs!*

* Literally, "Mr. Heaven," a colloquial
term for God.

67

Wise men, you have cast me aside.
Fools, I do the same to you.
I would be neither wise man nor fool;
From now on, let us hear no more from each other.
When night comes I sing to the bright moon;
At dawn, I dance with white clouds.
How could I still my voice and my hands
And sit stiff as a stick with my grey hair rumpled?

68

Would you know a simile for life and death?
Compare them then to water and ice.
Water binds together to become ice;
Ice melts and turns back into water.
What has died must live again,
What has been born shall return to death.
Water and ice do no harm to each other;
Life and death are both of them good.

69

Men these days search for a way through
                    the clouds,
But the cloud way is dark and without sign.
The mountains are high and often steep and rocky;
In the broadest valleys the sun seldom shines.
Green crests before you and behind,
White clouds to east and west—
Do you want to know where the cloud way lies?
There it is, in the midst of the Void!

70

Talking about food won't make you full,
Babbling of clothes won't keep out the cold.
A bowl of rice is what fills the belly;
It takes a suit of clothing to make you warm.
And yet, without stopping to consider this,
You complain that Buddha is hard to find.
Turn your mind within! There he is!
Why look for him abroad?

71

Living in the mountains, mind ill at ease,
All I do is grieve at the passing years.
At great labor I gathered the herbs of long life,
But has all my striving made me an immortal?
Broad is my garden and wrapped now in clouds,
But the woods are bright and the moon is full.
What am I doing here? Why don't I go home?
I am bound by the spell of the cinnamon trees!*

* The Chinese cinnamon trees of Mount
T'ien-t'ai are often mentioned in earlier
literature. They were of great height,
green all year round, and were venerated
as symbols of immortal life.

72

My house is at the foot of the green cliff,
My garden, a jumble of weeds I no longer bother
to mow.
New vines dangle in twisted strands
Over old rocks rising steep and high.
Monkeys make off with the mountain fruits,
The white heron crams his bill with fish
from the pond,
While I, with a book or two of the immortals,*
Read under the trees—mumble, mumble.

* The Taoist philosophers, so called because Taoism claimed to teach the art of becoming immortal.

73

Someone criticized the Master of Cold Mountain:
"Your poems make no sense at all!"
"But from what I have read of the ancients,"
                    I said,
"They weren't ashamed to be poor and humble . . ."
He laughed at my words and answered,
"How can you talk such foolishness?"
Then go on, my friend, as you are today.
Let money be your whole life for you!

74

The greatest sages from ancient times
Have not shown us life immortal.
What is born in time must die;
All will be changed to dust and ashes.
Bones pile up like Mount Vipula,*
Tears of parting would make a sea,
And all that's left are empty names.
Who escapes the wheel of birth and death?

* A mountain in India.

75

I wanted to go off to the eastern cliff—
How many years now I've planned the trip?
Yesterday I pulled myself up by the vines,
But wind and fog forced me to stop halfway.
The path was narrow and my clothes kept catching,
The moss so spongy I couldn't move my feet,
So I stopped under this red cinnamon tree.
I guess I'll lay my head on a cloud and sleep.

76

Here are four or five young fools!
Nothing they do is honest or true.
They've scarcely scanned ten volumes,
Yet their brushes are always ready with a
                        caustic comment.
They take up the "Rules for Confucian Behavior"
And pronounce it no better than a code for
                        thieves—
A species of pest like the silverfish
That chews through the binding of other men's
                        books.

* A section of the *Book of Rites* outlin-
ing the behavior appropriate to a Confucian gentleman. In Han-shan's time,
the Buddhists, Taoists, and Confucians
were constantly engaged in bitter attacks on each other. The poem is a satire
on ignorant Buddhist priests who spend
their time deriding other creeds.

77

What a fine shop this is!
And the wine they sell is the best around.
Bright banners flying on high;*
Pint or gallon, the measure is always fair.
What's that? You complain your sales are poor?
But then, you *will* keep the place full of
                              vicious dogs!
No sooner has a fellow come in for a drink
Than they snap at his heels and drive him away.†

* "Wine banners" advertising the shop.
† The parable of the dogs in the wine shop is very old in Chinese literature and originally referred to evil ministers who drive good men out of the government. Here I suspect it is an attack on the Buddhist clergy, though this is only a guess.

78

How pleasant were our bodies in the days of Chaos,
Needing neither to eat or piss!
Who came along with his drill
And bored us full of these nine holes?*
Morning after morning we must dress and eat;
Year after year, fret over taxes.
A thousand of us scrambling for a penny,
We knock our heads together and yell for dear life.

* In ancient times, according to the philosopher Chuang Tzu, the emperors of the northern and southern seas went to visit the emperor of the center, named Chaos. Having been generously entertained, they considered some way to repay their host's hospitality. "Everyone has seven holes in his body so that he can hear, see, breathe and eat," they remarked, "but Chaos doesn't seem to have any!" With this they began to bore holes in their host. Every day they bored another hole, and on the seventh day Chaos died. (*Chuang Tzu*, sec. 7.) Han-shan adds the two holes in the lower part of the body to make a total of nine.

79

On Cold Mountain lives a naked insect;
Its body is white and its head is black.
In its arm it carries a couple of books,
One "The Way" and the other "The Power."*
At home it doesn't bother with kettle or stove,
On a journey it takes along no clothes,
But always it carries the sword of True Wisdom
To cut down the thieves of senseless desire.

* The *Tao-te-ching* or "Classic of the
Way and Its Power" by the Taoist
philosopher Lao Tzu. In Han-shan's
time the work was divided into two
sections, as referred to in the poem.

80

Man, living in the dust,
Is like a bug trapped in a bowl.
All day he scrabbles round and round,
But never escapes from the bowl that holds him.
The immortals are beyond his reach,
His cravings have no end,
While months and years flow by like a river
Until, in an instant, he has grown old.

81

Often I have heard how Emperor Wu of the Han
And the First Emperor of the Ch'in before him
Delighted in tales of immortals and spirits
And tried in vain to prolong their lives.
Now their golden towers are broken,
Their palaces have vanished away,
While the grave at Mou-ling and the tomb of
                    Mount Li*
Are today a wilderness of weeds.

* Where Emperor Wu (reigned 140-87
B. C.) and the First Emperor (reigned
221-210 B. C.), respectively, were buried.

82

People ask the way to Cold Mountain.
Cold Mountain? There is no road that goes
      through.
Even in summer the ice doesn't melt;
Though the sun comes out, the fog is blinding.
How can you hope to get there by aping me?
Your heart and mine are not alike.
If your heart were the same as mine,
Then you could journey to the very center!

[handwritten annotations:]
No set path or pattern to follow
obstacles
Enlightenment

Sun is always shining, something blocks our way.
Fog of ignorance blocks & blinds

our hearts are different
If you were in touch with yourself
you could be here too.

83

[handwritten: Taoist kind of immortality]

The crane, with a twig of bitter peach in his bill,
Rested but once in thousand miles.
He wanted to go to the mountain of P'eng-lai,*
And the peach was to serve him as food on
         the way.
Still far from his goal, his feathers dropped off;
Parted from the flock, his heart grew sad.
And when he hurried home to his nest,
He found that his wife no longer knew him.

[handwritten: isolated — in exile. misses friends]

[handwritten: all the Taoist images]

[handwritten: Biographical]

* A legendary mountainous island in the
eastern sea where immortal spirits live.
The peach is the food of the immortals.

84

With mind as lofty as the mountain peak,
And self-righteous look ("Me bow to others?"),
He announces he will lecture on the Vedic canon,
Having mastered all the writings of the
                    Three Religions.*
In his heart there is no trace of shame,
Though he breaks the commandments and
                    ignores the holy laws.
"My sermons are for men of superior
                    understanding.
Few are the priests who can compare with me!"
Fools all shower him with praise,
While wise men clap their hands in mirth.
This hoax! This phantom flower of the air!
How could he escape from birth and death?
Better to understand nothing at all,
To sit still and quiet the ills of the mind.

* Buddhism, Taoism, and Confucianism.

85

I came once to sit on Cold Mountain
And lingered here for thirty years.
Yesterday I went to see relatives and friends;
Over half had gone to the Yellow Springs.
Bit by bit life fades like a guttering lamp,
Passes on like a river that never rests.
This morning I face my lonely shadow
And before I know it tears stream down.

86

The clear water sparkles like crystal,
You can see through it easily, right to the bottom.
My mind is free from every thought,
Nothing in the myriad realms can move it.
Since it cannot be wantonly roused,
Forever and forever it will stay unchanged.
When you have learned to know in this way,
You will know there is no inside or out!*

* That is, no duality.

87

Buddhist priests don't keep the commandments,
Taoists don't take their immortality pills.
Lots of wise men have lived since ancient times,
And there they lie, under the green hill.

88

By chance I happened to visit an eminent priest
Among the mist-wrapped mountains piled
           peak on peak.
As he pointed out for me the road home,
The moon hung out its single round lamp.

89

In my house there is a cave,*
And in the cave is nothing at all—
Pure and wonderfully empty,
Resplendent, with a light like the sun.
A meal of greens will do for this old body,
A ragged coat will cover this phantom form.
Let a thousand saints appear before me—
I have the Buddha of Heavenly Truth!

* The cave of the mind.

90

All your days are like a drunken stupor,
But the flowing years never for a moment
                stand still.
When you're buried under the weed-grown turf,
How black will be the moon that shines
                down there!
When bones and flesh have rotted and scattered
And the spirit is fading away,*
Then, had you jaws that would bite through iron,
How could you intone your Taoist scriptures?

* According to Chinese belief, the spirit
does not die immediately with the body,
but only gradually fades away into
nothing.

91

Body clothed in a no-cloth robe,
Feet clad in turtle's fur boots,
I seize my bow of rabbit horn
And prepare to shoot the devil Ignorance.

92

Today I sat before the cliff,
Sat a long time till mists had cleared.
A single thread, the clear stream runs cold;
A thousand yards the green peaks lift their heads.
White clouds—the morning light is still;
Moonrise—the lamp of night drifts upward;
Body free from dust and stain,
What cares could trouble my mind?

93

Here is a tree older than the forest itself;
The years of its life defy reckoning.
Its roots have seen the upheavals of hill and valley,
Its leaves have known the changes of
                wind and frost.
The world laughs at its shoddy exterior
And cares nothing for the fine grain
                of the wood inside.
Stripped free of flesh and hide,
All that remains is the core of truth.*

* When a monk asked the Zen Master
Ma-tsu what enlightenment he had
achieved, he replied,
   "Stripping away all flesh and hide,
   I have only a single truth."
(*Ma-tsu yü-lu*, in *Ssu-chia yü-lu*.)

94

All my life I have been lazy,
Hating anything solemn, finding light matters
                more congenial.
Others may study how to make a profit,
I have my single roll of scripture.*
I do not bother to fit it with roller or case,
Or trouble to carry it here and there.
Like a doctor prescribing a medicine
                for each disease,
I use what remedy is at hand to save the world.
Only when the mind is free of care
Can the light of understanding shine
                in every corner.

* A metaphor for the "single truth" of
the preceding poem.

95

Now I have a single robe,*
Not made of gauze or of figured silk.
Do you ask what color it is?
Not crimson, nor purple either.
Summer days I wear it as a cloak,
In winter it serves for a quilt.
Summer and winter in turn I use it;
Year after year, only this.

* Again a metaphor for the "single truth."

96

Have I a body or have I none?
Am I who I am or am I not?
Pondering these questions,
I sit leaning against the cliff while the
                   years go by,
Till the green grass grows between my feet
And the red dust settles on my head,
And the men of the world, thinking me dead,
Come with offerings of wine and fruit
                 to lay by my corpse.

97

My mind is like the autumn moon
Shining clean and clear in the green pool.
No, that's not a good comparison.
Tell me, how shall I explain?

98

In the late sun I descended the western hill,
Light streaming over the grass and trees,
Till I came to a dark and gloomy place
Where pines and creepers grew thick together.
Within crouched many tigers;
When they saw me, their fur stood on end.
Not so much as a knife in my hand,
Did I not gasp with fear?

99

So Han-shan writes you these words,
These words which no one will believe.
Honey is sweet; men love the taste.
Medicine is bitter and hard to swallow.
What soothes the feelings brings contentment,
What opposes the will calls forth anger.
Yet I ask you to look at the wooden puppets,
Worn out by their moment of play on stage!

100

Do you have the poems of Han-shan in your house?
They're better for you than sutra-reading!
Write them out and paste them on a screen
Where you can glance them over from time to time.